TIME
FOR KIDS

WILD
CITIES

Timothy J. Bradley

Consultant

Timothy Rasinski, Ph.D.
Kent State University

Lori Oczkus
Literacy Consultant

Tejdeep Kochhar
High School Biology Teacher

Publishing Credits

Dona Herweck Rice, *Editor-in-Chief*
Lee Aucoin, *Creative Director*
Jamey Acosta, *Senior Editor*
Lexa Hoang, *Designer*
Stephanie Reid, *Photo Editor*
Rane Anderson, *Contributing Author*
Rachelle Cracchiolo, M.S.Ed., *Publisher*

Image Credits: pp.25 (bottom), p.38 (right), p.39 (bottom) Getty Images; pp.10–11, 22, 35, 48 Timothy J. Bradley; pp.16–17, Courtney Patterson; p.35 (top) iStockphoto; p.34 EPA/Newscom; pp.15, 18–19 (bottom), pp.32–33 Photo Researchers, Inc.; all other images Shutterstock.

Teacher Created Materials

5301 Oceanus Drive
Huntington Beach, CA 92649-1030
http://www.tcmpub.com

ISBN 978-1-4333-4823-5

© 2013 Teacher Created Materials, Inc.

TABLE OF CONTENTS

Cities in Nature 4

Insect Cities. 6

Mammal Cities 20

Miniature Cities 30

A Wild World 40

Glossary 42

Index 44

Bibliography 46

More to Explore 47

About the Author. 48

CITIES IN NATURE

A city is a place where many people live together. Cities have everything humans need for work, play, and survival. And cities can be very fun places to live.

Humans aren't the only animals that build cities. Some animals live in large groups that are like human cities. Animals that live together can watch out for one another. They can sound a warning when there is danger. It's easier to find food and care for babies when there's help.

In cozy rabbit **warrens**, busy beehives, and action-packed **anthills**, animals live together. The world is full of wild cities.

Meerkats live in groups.

New York City is the largest human city in America. Over 8 million people live there.

Thousands of ants live in and below one anthill.

THINK LINK

- In what ways do you think animal communities are like human cities?

- What do you think are the advantages of living in a city?

- How can we learn from the way animals build their cities?

INSECT CITIES

Some insects live together in groups. Thousands of ants share a single **anthill.** Hundreds of hornets may live in one nest. Together, they can find food. In large numbers, they can defend the **colony** against attacks.

Insects that live together are **eusocial**. Eusocial insects **evolved** to build complex cities. The ancestors of these insects that lived alone died easily. Those that worked together lived longer. For ants, wasps, and termites, living together means survival.

bees covering their hive

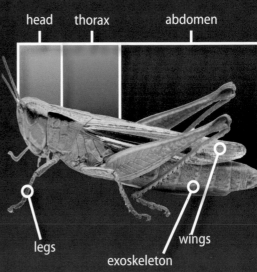

By climbing on each other, ants work together to form a bridge between two leaves.

Insect Basics

head   thorax   abdomen

An insect is a type of **arthropod**. Insects have an **exoskeleton**, segmented body, and jointed legs. Their bodies are divided into three parts: head, thorax, and abdomen. They have wings and three pairs of legs.

legs

exoskeleton

wings

INSIDE THE HIVE

Honeybees build cities in the form of hives. A beehive is where bees make honey and raise their young. Worker bees fly away from the hive to look for flowers and gather **pollen** and nectar. They bring the pollen and nectar back to the hive. That is where nectar is made into honey. The bee **larvae** eat the honey. Worker bees do a dance to tell other bees where to find the flowers.

The honeycombs inside the hive are made up of six-sided **cells**. Bees eat the honey. They change the sugar into wax. The bees chew the flakes of wax until they soften. Then the bees use the wax to build more cells in the hive.

a bee collecting nectar

Building Without a Plan

Instincts are actions that animals are born knowing how to perform. Instincts tell an animal to hunt. Instincts tell an animal to find a mate. Instincts drive tiny insects to work together to build a large home for themselves.

an enormous termite mound

Some types of bees live alone. These solitary bees do not live as long as bees that live in groups.

Colony Collapse Disorder

Imagine you lived in a big city. How would you feel if you found out most other people had vanished? It sounds like some kind of horror story. But this is what is happening to bee colonies around the world. Worker bees are disappearing from their hives, and the hives can't function without them. Scientists are still puzzled by these disappearances, which they call *colony collapse disorder*.

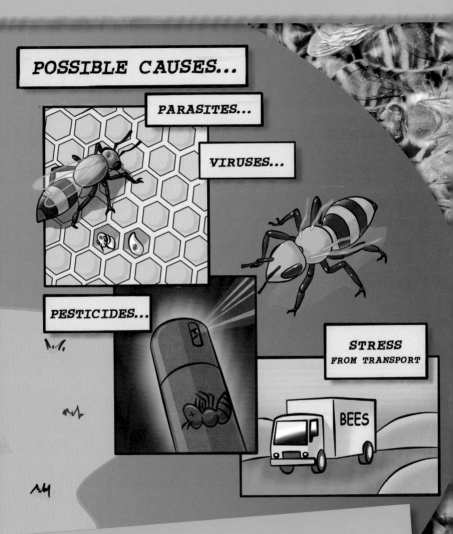

Division of Labor

In a city, everyone has a role. A colony of bees is divided into several different types of bees. The queen is the most important bee in the colony. She lays the eggs that will become the worker bees. The workers care for the larvae and feed the queen. **Drones** are male bees. They mate with the queen. In the fall, the drones are forced from the hive and die.

THE HORNET'S NEST

Hornets are eusocial insects. As many as 700 hornets may live in one nest. They work together so there will be enough food for everyone. Hornets work together to protect the nest, too.

To make a new nest, the queen finds a safe place. She chews tree bark to soften it. The chewed bark is used to make six-sided cells. These cells are the base of the nest. The queen lays an egg in each cell. After the larvae hatch, they will grow into adults. As adults, they will help to make the nest bigger.

Gardeners are happy to see hornets in their garden. Hornets keep away insects that are harmful to crops.

a hornet eating a caterpillar

Hornets are a type of wasp. Wasps are known as the first paper makers. When the bark is chewed to create the nest, it resembles gray paper.

Sound the Alarm

Hornets are very protective of their nests. Hornets sting their prey and any creature that threatens the hive.

INSIDE THE ANTHILL

Ants are also eusocial. Thousands work to build underground nests in the dirt. Their tunneling makes a lot of loose soil. The ants remove the soil. They pile it outside an entry hole, which makes a small hill, called an *anthill*.

Ants divide up the work of the colony. There is a job for every kind of ant. Worker ants look for food and dig tunnels. Soldier ants protect the colony from attack. There may be several ant queens in one nest. These queens lay eggs and help the colony grow.

soldier ants

Ancient Ants

Ants first appeared on Earth during the **Cretaceous period**, over 100 million years ago. Since then, ants have colonized nearly every place on Earth.

Thousands of ants follow each other to a new food source.

Supercolonies

Often, ant colonies are seen attacking each other. However, some ant colonies will work together and form a huge supercolony. Supercolonies have been seen in many places around the world. One supercolony in Europe is almost 4,000 miles long!

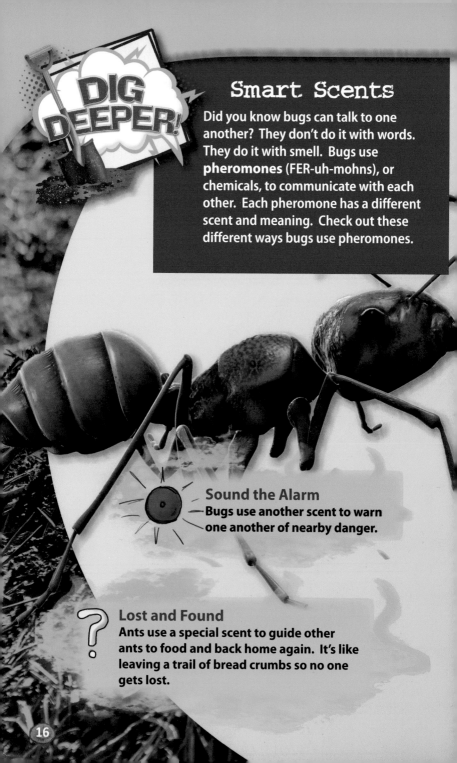

DIG DEEPER!

Smart Scents

Did you know bugs can talk to one another? They don't do it with words. They do it with smell. Bugs use **pheromones** (FER-uh-mohns), or chemicals, to communicate with each other. Each pheromone has a different scent and meaning. Check out these different ways bugs use pheromones.

Sound the Alarm
Bugs use another scent to warn one another of nearby danger.

Lost and Found
Ants use a special scent to guide other ants to food and back home again. It's like leaving a trail of bread crumbs so no one gets lost.

Hey! Get a whiff of this!

Yoo-hoo!
Some pheromones are used to attract mates or lure prey.

To-Do List
Some pheromones communicate the tasks that need to be done, like grooming the queen.

Trash Pickup
Insects can use pheromones to find an insect that has died and needs to be removed from the colony.

ANT WARS

Unlike other ants, army ants don't build nests. During the day, they form long lines as they look for food. They work together to capture and kill anything in their path. Army ants use their strong jaws and stingers to kill prey. A large group of army ants can overwhelm an animal as large as a small lizard. At night, they make a "nest" with their bodies. They hook their legs together to form a huge **bivouac** (BIV-oo-ak).

army ants carrying their prey

The Same but Different

Most ants build underground nests. They spend a lot of time and energy digging and taking care of the nest. But army ants huddle together to form their bivouac. This saves energy.

Living Raft

Army ants can cross water by linking together to form a raft. Some ants will drown, but millions in the colony will survive.

19

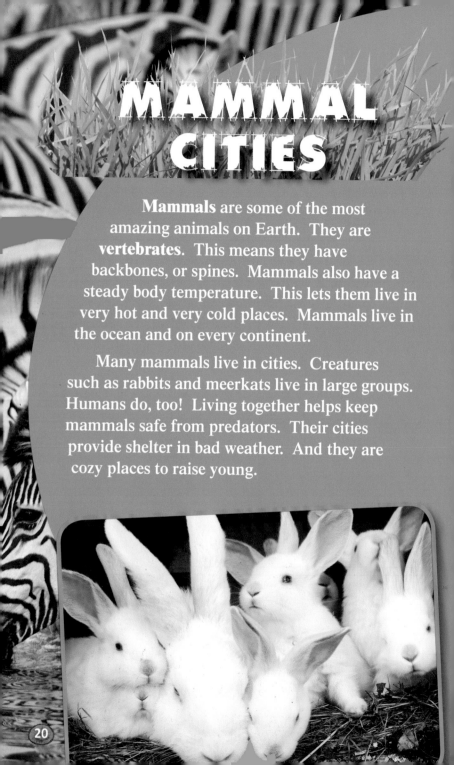

MAMMAL CITIES

Mammals are some of the most amazing animals on Earth. They are **vertebrates**. This means they have backbones, or spines. Mammals also have a steady body temperature. This lets them live in very hot and very cold places. Mammals live in the ocean and on every continent.

Many mammals live in cities. Creatures such as rabbits and meerkats live in large groups. Humans do, too! Living together helps keep mammals safe from predators. Their cities provide shelter in bad weather. And they are cozy places to raise young.

Mammal Basics

Mammals are warm-blooded vertebrates. They feed milk to their young, and their skin is usually covered with hair. Humans, mice, and whales are all mammals.

Not all animals live in cities. Some animals, including adult tigers without cubs, live alone.

TIME LINE: THE RISE OF CITIES

400 million years ago
The first plants evolve on land.
The first insects arrive.

Over 100 million years ago
Ants begin digging tunneled cities underground.

200 million years ago
Mammals begin competing with dinosaurs.

300 million years ago
Reptiles begin to dominate life on Earth.

Roughly 4 billion years ago
Life on Earth begins in the sea.

Today

More people live in Seoul, South Korea than in any other city. It's home to more than 10 million people.

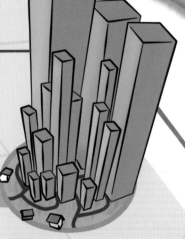

100,000 years ago
Modern humans appear.

8,000 years ago
The first human cities appear.

23 million years ago
Mammals grow more complex.

STOP! THINK...

- Look at the time line. When did changes happen most quickly?

- Why do you think it took humans so long to develop cities?

- What do you think will happen next?

40 million years ago
Rabbits begin to build underground cities.

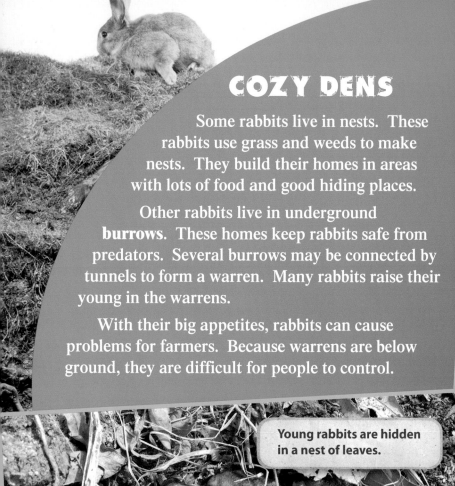

COZY DENS

Some rabbits live in nests. These rabbits use grass and weeds to make nests. They build their homes in areas with lots of food and good hiding places.

Other rabbits live in underground **burrows**. These homes keep rabbits safe from predators. Several burrows may be connected by tunnels to form a warren. Many rabbits raise their young in the warrens.

With their big appetites, rabbits can cause problems for farmers. Because warrens are below ground, they are difficult for people to control.

Young rabbits are hidden in a nest of leaves.

As many as 20 rabbits can live in a warren.

Life Underground

Rabbits dig tunnels underground to stay safe and dry. Humans build subway tunnels under large cities to make it easier to travel from place to place.

MEERKAT MANSION

Meerkats are small mammals that live in Africa. They live in groups of up to 25. Meerkats can dig through sand very quickly. Working together, they build underground colonies. These are connected by tunnels. During the day, meerkats hunt. They eat insects and snakes. Meerkats work together to care for their young and find food.

The colony also works together to avoid predators. They spend much of their time above ground. But they can run underground whenever they are threatened. The **sentry** is in charge of watching for danger. When the sentry senses danger, it lets out a sharp bark. This warns the other meerkats. The sentry is the first one out of the burrow. It lets the others know it is safe to go back outside.

A sentry stands tall, watching for danger.

Who's Who

Every meerkat colony is made up of meerkats with different roles.

These two meerkats control the others.

Alpha Male　　　**Alpha Female**

Beta Males and Females

Most meerkats are betas and follow the alphas. When they are three years old, they leave and try to start a new colony.

Pups　　　**Babysitters**　　　**Sentry**

Young meerkats are pups for 10 months. They live underground for protection.

The babysitters care for the pups while the other adults search for food.

The sentry watches for danger and lets the others know when it's safe to return to the tunnels.

DIG DEEPER!

Moving Cities

Many animals live in groups, but not all these animals build cities. Many animals travel in herds. A herd protects the animals as they travel to find food and water. Adults can lead large numbers of young into new places.

Some herds **migrate** great distances, returning to the same places each year to find resources. Over 10 billion locusts migrate in a single **swarm**. Billions of birds migrate together each year. Mammals such as sheep, zebras, lions, and elephants all travel in groups.

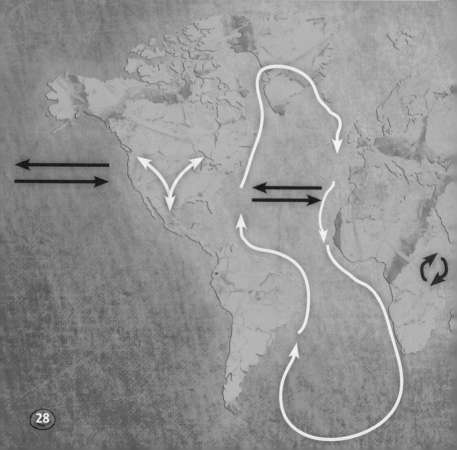

 bluefin tuna

 Arctic tern

 Monarch butterfly

 wildebeest

 bar-tailed godwit

Globe Trekkers

You know when you see a group of birds it's called a *flock of birds*. But what is it called when you see a group of lions? Check out these animal groups to see how many you already know.

army of ants

flutter of butterflies

herd of deer

pack of dogs

pride of lions

nest of mice

bed of oysters

prickle of porcupines

knot of snakes

MINIATURE CITIES

Even very small creatures can live in cities. Imagine a moving city of slime. We may not usually notice such tiny **organisms**. But when they join together, they can create huge homes that we can't miss. These **microscopic** organisms live together in groups that make it easier to catch food and stay safe. None of these organisms has a brain. But they can work together. Then, they act like a single, much smarter organism.

mold on wood

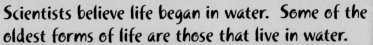

Scientists believe life began in water. Some of the oldest forms of life are those that live in water.

coral

What's a Microbe?

The word *microbe* is a combination of two Greek words. *Micro* describes very small things. *Bio* means *life*. Microbes include bacteria, viruses, fungi, and some algae. It's a catch-all term for life that can only be seen under the microscope.

Mushrooms are a form of fungus.

UNDERWATER SYMPHONY

The snapping shrimp is a brown-and-white shrimp. It makes its home in tide pools and muddy waters. The shrimp live together in colonies of 30 to 100 individuals. Every snapping shrimp is nearly blind. Together, they dig holes in sand and mud to hide from predators.

The snapping shrimp has two claws. One is small and pointed. The other is fatter and shaped like a boxing glove. The shrimp catches prey in its large claw. As the claw shoots forward, the water forms a bubble. The bubble pops. This makes a sharp cracking sound. When large numbers of shrimp snap their claws, it makes one of the loudest sounds in the ocean! The shrimp use the sound to communicate and defend the colony.

snapping shrimp

Roommates

Many snapping shrimp share their homes with goby fish. This is a **symbiotic** relationship, which means both species benefit. The shrimp builds the burrow. The goby has better vision and watches for danger. The goby shivers to warn the shrimp of danger.

The sound the snapping shrimp makes stuns its prey. Then, the shrimp can take apart the animal and eat it.

ARMY OF MEN

With their long **tentacles**, Portuguese man-of-wars look like jellyfish. But these are not jellyfish. They aren't even individual animals. A man-of-war is a group of tiny animals working together to survive. The man-of-war is made of four types of **polyps.** A polyp filled with gas acts like the sail on a boat. This helps the man-of-war move. Underwater, some polyps sting attackers and defend the colony. There are polyps that make new polyps. There are also feeding polyps. They break down the food captured by the stinging polyps.

a Portuguese man-of-war washed up on the beach

Stinging Surprise

Touching a man-of-war is very painful. If you're at the beach, take care to avoid these creatures. They can be dangerous for weeks after they die on the beach. If you do get stung, visit a doctor right away!

Living Sailboat

The gas-filled "sail" of the man-of-war keeps it on the surface of the water. The sail can be deflated when the man-of-war needs to dive under water to avoid an attack.

The gas-filled polyp helps move the colony.

The reproductive polyp makes new polyps.

Feeding polyps digest food.

Stinging polyps capture food for the colony.

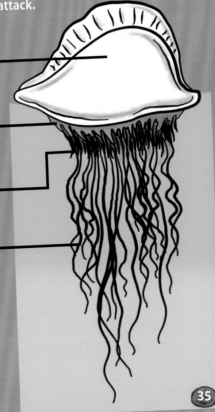

35

CORAL CITY

Stony coral are tiny organisms that live in warm oceans around the world. The coral catch microbes and small fish with their stinging tentacles. Each coral is very tiny. But they live together in huge groups.

Stony coral are clear. With algae, they create a hard exoskeleton to protect themselves. The algae add bright colors to the exoskeleton. A coral colony can grow for thousands of years. People travel around the world to admire these amazing structures.

Coral live in oceans around the world and can be found as deep as 20,000 feet.

Exoskeleton City

Coral reefs can stretch for miles. The Great Barrier Reef off the coast of Australia covers 133,000 square miles. It is one of the seven natural wonders of the world.

Cities in Danger

Coral is very sensitive to environmental changes. As human activity warms the Earth, coral may not survive the changes. Beautiful coral cities all around the world are in danger of dying.

CITIES OF ICK

Imagine an orange puddle of slime. It might not look like it, but these tiny organisms form a slimy city. Slime molds are colonies of **protists**. They look just the way they sound—like lumps of slime! The slime is thick like oatmeal. It can have very bright colors. Some are bright yellow or pink. Slime molds are often found on the ground in forests where it is cold and wet. They feed on the microbes found on dead plants. The slime rolls along on the forest floor until it finds something to eat.

Slime molds are made up of tiny creatures. Alone, they have no real intelligence. But when they form a colony, a slime mold can do some interesting things. When a slime mold is cut into several pieces, the pieces can find their way back together again. Scientists don't understand how the slime mold knows to do this. It doesn't have any kind of brain.

Ask the Slime Mold

Slime molds may lack brains, but they are experts at finding the shortest and fastest way to travel between two points. Scientists are studying slime molds to see if they can teach us how to build better subway systems.

Slime molds can be found all over the world in all different colors.

A WILD WORLD

Honk! Honk! Move aside! There's work to do here! Around the world, tunnels are being dug. Food is being stored. Young are being raised. And homes are being protected. Deep in the earth and high in the sky, animals have built some of the most fascinating cities in the world.

GLOSSARY

anthill—a small pile of dirt or sand marking the entrance to an ant colony

arthropod—an animal with a body in three parts, jointed limbs, and an exoskeleton

bivouac—a temporary shelter formed by a resting colony of army ants

burrows—holes or tunnels made in the ground by an animal for shelter

cells—small spaces; compartments in a hive

colony—a group of animals of the same type living together

Colony Collapse Disorder—a mysterious disease that causes bees to leave their hive

Cretaceous period—the time period between 145 and 65 million years ago

drone—a male honeybee

eusocial—organisms that live as a group or colony

evolved—changed over time, adapted to new conditions

exoskeleton—a hard protective structure on the outside of the body

instincts—natural, automatic abilities and responses

larvae—young wingless insects, often shaped like worms

mammals—warm-blooded vertebrate animals

microscopic—able to be seen only through a microscope

migrate—to pass from one region to another on a regular schedule for feeding or mating

organisms—individual living things

pheromones—chemicals that can be smelled by animals and act as a signal to other animals

pollen—a yellow, powdery substance produced by plants in order to reproduce

polyps—small invertebrates; may live alone or in colonies

protists—simple microorganisms

sentry—a guard or watcher

supercolony—several colonies that join together into one big one

swarm—a large number of something, usually in motion

symbiotic—when two different types of organisms live together and both benefit

tentacles—long, flexible legs or arms on an animal, used for feeling and grasping

vertebrates—animals that have backbones

warrens—underground communities of burrows joined together by tunnels

INDEX

Africa, 26

algae, 31, 36

America, 5

ant, 6–7, 14–15, 16, 18–19, 22, 29

anthill, 4, 6, 14

Arctic tern, 29

army ants, 18–19

arthropod, 7

Australia, 37

bacteria, 31

bar-tailed godwit, 29

bee, 6–11, 17

birds, 28–29

bivouac, 18–19

bluefin tuna, 29

burrow, 24, 26, 33

butterflies, 29

colony, 6, 10–11, 14–15, 17, 19, 26–27, 32, 34–36, 38

colony collapse disorder, 10

coral, 31, 36–37

Cretaceous period, 15

deer, 29

dinosaurs, 22

dogs, 29

drones, 11

Earth, 15, 20, 22, 37

elephants, 28

eusocial, 6–7, 12, 14

exoskeleton, 7, 36–37

fungus, 31

gardeners, 12

goby fish, 33

Great Barrier Reef, 37

herds, 28

hive, 8, 10–11, 13

honey, 8

hornets, 6, 12–13

humans, 4–5, 20–21, 23, 25

insect, 6–7, 12, 17, 22, 26

instincts, 9

jellyfish, 34

larvae, 8, 11, 12

lions, 28–29

lizard, 18

locusts, 28

mammal, 20–23, 26, 28

meerkats, 4, 20, 26–27

mice, 21, 29

microbes, 31, 36, 38

mold, 30, 38–39

Monarch butterfly, 29

nectar, 8

nest, 6, 12–14, 18–19, 24, 29

New York City, 5

oysters, 29

parasite, 11

pesticides, 11

pheromones, 16–17

plants, 22, 38

pollen, 8

polyps, 34–35

porcupines, 29

Portuguese man-of-wars, 34–35

predators, 20, 24, 26, 32

protists, 38

queen, 11, 12, 14, 17

rabbit, 4, 20, 23–25

reef, 37

reptiles, 22

sentry, 26–27

Seoul, South Korea, 23

sheep, 28

slime mold, 38–39

snakes, 29

snapping shrimp, 32–33

supercolony, 15

swarm, 28

termites, 6–7, 9

tigers, 21

tunnels, 14, 24, 25, 27, 40

vertebrates, 20–21

viruses, 11, 31

warrens, 4, 24–25

wasp, 6–7, 13

whales, 21

wildebeest, 29

zebras, 28

BIBLIOGRAPHY

Carney, Elizabeth. *Great Migrations: Whales, Wildebeests, Butterflies, Elephants, and Other Amazing Animals on the Move.* National Geographic Children's Books, 2010.

This book tells the stories of many different animal migrations, from whales to butterflies. Each shows the strength of the animals and their will to survive.

Markovics, Joyce L. *The Honey Bee's Hive: A Thriving City.* Bearport Pub., 2010.

The hive of a honeybee is an extremely busy place. In this book, learn all about how bees work together in their home.

Rhodes, Mary Jo, and David Hall. *Life on a Coral Reef.* Children's Press, 2007.

Explore life on a coral reef and learn all about the fragile balance of climate and wildlife that make life on a reef possible.

Robinson, W. Wright. *Animal Architects: How Mammals Build Their Amazing Homes.* Blackbirch Press, 1999.

Mammals build homes to raise their young or live in communities. This book tells all about how they construct their homes. You'll learn about beavers, chimpanzees, squirrels, moles, badgers, and more.

MORE TO EXPLORE

Bio Kids

http://www.biokids.umich.edu/guides/tracks_and_sign/build

This webpage provides links to information on many of the different homes that insects and animals build, including webs, cocoons, nests, burrows, and more.

Kidport Reference Library

http://www.kidport.com/reflib/science/animalhomes/animalhomes.htm

This webpage provides links to various home types, such as caves, hives, nests, and more, and tells which types of animals live in those homes.

National Geographic for Kids

http://kids.nationalgeographic.com/kids/

National Geographic's website for kids provides information on a variety of wildlife and provides photos and videos of landscapes from around the world, as well as games and other activities.

Teacher Tube

http://teachertube.com

Teachertube.com is a safe website for teachers to look up videos to use in their classrooms to support whatever content you're are studying—including animals.

ABOUT THE AUTHOR

Timothy J. Bradley grew up near Boston, Massachusetts, and spent every spare minute drawing spaceships, robots, and dinosaurs. He enjoyed it so much that he started writing and illustrating books about natural history and science fiction. Timothy also worked as a toy designer for Hasbro, Inc., and designed life-size dinosaurs for museum exhibits. Timothy loves looking at bugs and the amazing things they can build.

Timothy lives in sunny Southern California with his wife and son.